BUSINESS
of
CHURCH

THE CONCISE
BUSINESS HANDBOOK
FOR PASTORS

STEPHEN D. LENTZ, ESQ.

HIGH BRIDGE BOOKS
HOUSTON

The Business of Church
by Stephen D. Lentz, Esq.

Printed in the United States of America
ISBN (Paperback): 978-1-946615-72-5
ISBN (eBook): 978-1-946615-32-9

High Bridge Books titles may be purchased in bulk for educational, business, fundraising, or sales promotional use. For information, please contact High Bridge Books via www.HighBridgeBooks.com/contact.

Published in Houston, Texas by High Bridge Books

CONTENTS

———— ❖ ————

Pastors,
You Need This Book!

---◈---

THE LAST TIME I checked, most pastors did not enter the ministry with an MBA, nor did they intend to get an MBA as a result of their calling to pastor a church. A good friend works with burned out pastors all over the nation.[1] He regularly gives them a survey inquiring why they entered the ministry. The overwhelming majority of pastors entered the ministry to "help people" and "preach the word of God." This is not surprising. What is surprising is that 80% to 90% of the time spent in ministry has nothing to do with either of these noble desires.

Most of a pastor's time is spent managing "The Business of Church." Some do this adequately, some excel in this area, but the vast majority fail miserably. According to Dr. Scalise, the day-in-and-day-out failure of this part of the ministry builds up over time and eventually manifests itself in some form of defeated or aberrant behavior… sexual misconduct, malfeasance, addictive behavior, and worse. *Seminary does not teach business principles.* Our pastors are ill-equipped to handle the day-to-day pressures and responsibilities of real "ministry."

---

[1] Dr. Eric Scalise.

PUT ON THE
WHOLE ARMOR OF GOD!

AS AN ORDAINED PASTOR and as a complex business law attorney, I have the privilege of understanding the pressures of ministry in a unique way.

In my corporate expertise, I have the privilege of representing churches in every state in the United States and in all the provinces of Canada. Qualifying as probably one of five church law authorities in North America, I have a macro-vision of what God is doing across a continent. I have the privilege of working with virtually all of the mainline denominations, as well as the existing world of emerging church movements like Hillsong, Planetshakers, ARC, and C-3 churches.

As an ordained pastor, working with my church in Virginia Beach, Virginia[1] on a weekly basis, I have the privilege of working on a micro-basis with real people facing real issues and life pressures.

Paul, in writing to the church in Ephesus, was "reading our mail." He writes:

> God is strong, and he wants you strong. So take everything the Master has set out for you, well-made weapons of the best materials. And put them to use so you will be able to stand up to everything the Devil throws your way. This is no afternoon athletic contest that we'll walk away from and

forget about in a couple of hours. This is for keeps, a life-or-death fight to the finish against the Devil and all his angels. Be prepared. You're up against far more than you can handle on your own. Take all the help you can get, every weapon God has issued…

(Eph. 6:10–14a MSG)

I live in a military community in Hampton Roads, Virginia. Our region has the privilege of being the headquarters for the Atlantic Fleet, Oceana Air Base, and Seal Team Six, as well as Fort Eustis, Camp Perry, and the Quantico base for the Marines. It is not difficult in my hometown to understand how important it is to use *all of the equipment* that has been masterfully designed for our military to give us the superiority that we enjoy. How absurd to think that any soldier in their right mind would only use part of the equipment issued to them. *Every piece* has been created to protect them and give them an advantage in battle. *Every piece* is uniquely designed to win the battle.

The preaching might be great, the worship and music awesome, the venue decked out beautifully, but the business and legal end of things is in disarray!

Our churches are in a more important battle. We are in a "life-or-death fight to the finish against the Devil and all his angels." Yet our churches and pastors find themselves accessing only *part* of the armor available to them. The preaching might be great, the worship and music awesome, the venue decked out beautifully, but *the business and legal end of things is in disarray.*

We can put on the "whole armor of God"… "every weapon God has issued."

Part of that armor is knowing and understanding our legal rights and the structuring that is available to us as churches and pastors. This book is designed to highlight the basics that every pastor needs to be aware of to fully position his/her church to take all of the ground that God has given them in their community.

---

[1] CrossWalk Virginia Beach: www.CrossWalk.cc

It's Not Unspiritual to Know and Use Your Legal Rights

The Incorporation Shield

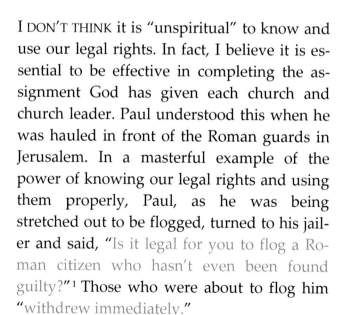

I DON'T THINK it is "unspiritual" to know and use our legal rights. In fact, I believe it is essential to be effective in completing the assignment God has given each church and church leader. Paul understood this when he was hauled in front of the Roman guards in Jerusalem. In a masterful example of the power of knowing our legal rights and using them properly, Paul, as he was being stretched out to be flogged, turned to his jailer and said, "Is it legal for you to flog a Roman citizen who hasn't even been found guilty?"[1] Those who were about to flog him "withdrew immediately."

Because he understood his legal rights, his ministry was extended. He would later be martyred, but not on that day!

Creating the right structure around the church can protect the church, as well as the pastor or its leaders, from massive exposure!

I believe we are living in a period of "extension." God is granting the church precious time to continue to take ground for the gospel of Jesus Christ. But that extension vitally depends on the church being more intentional and informed than ever before in the area of business, finance, and the law.

We do not live in a friendly world. God has called us to reach out to the whole world but not to be seduced by it or ignorant of its ways.[2]

One of the most important pieces of armor we have today is corporate law. It is a shield against liability.

Creating the right structure around the church can protect the church, as well as the pastor or its leaders, from massive exposure! Most churches begin their existence as unincorporated associations. The church starts in a home, migrates to borrowed or rented facilities, and, eventually, finds a place of its own. During the early years, the legal structure is not a dominant part of the thinking. The dominant thought is to survive. But remaining unincorporated has many shortcomings, which can eventually expose the church and the leaders to unnecessary risks.

---

*In my opinion, the unincorporated association status is the **most intrusive format** a church can choose!*

The usual argument I hear from unincorporated churches is, "We don't want the state involved in our church's business."

The problem is *the state is already involved in the church's business!* The classification as an unincorporated church comes from your state code. *The state* has decided how you will be regulated under this code. *The state* has prescribed the rules and regulations for the church's liability and accountability under the Unincorporated Association Statutes or the Religious Unincorporated Act.

In my opinion, the unincorporated association status is the *most intrusive format* a church can choose. In some extreme cases, the pastor, elders, and trustees can be held personally liable for the debts and liabilities of the church. Each can be jointly and severally liable. And talk about intrusive, the court must approve any decision to buy, sell, or encumber property held by the church. Even if the pastor, elders, trustees, and congregation *all decide* to sell a piece of church property, the court still needs to give permission for the activity under an unincorporated association format.

By choosing to incorporate, the church can *govern itself* under its bylaws. Decisions can be made by the officers and directors of the church under the polity of that particular church. The bylaws govern. There is no personal liability for the pastor and directors.[3] The church is free to identify its role in the community and follow God's leading based on its own mission and purpose. Incorporating the local church is probably one of the most basic and important maneuvers a pastor can make to protect his/her church and position it to last over time. Incorporation is a "shield"—an essential piece of the whole armor of God available to the church!

---

[1] Acts 22:22-29

[2] Matthew 10:16

[3] No person is ever indemnified for malfeasance or criminal activity. However, as long as the officers and directors are using the "business judgment rule" and making responsible decisions with proper due diligence, there is no personal liability.

ARMOR 2

DON'T BORROW EQUIPMENT!

Beware of the Cut-and-Paste Mentality

I HAVE MET so many church leaders who have bylaws but have no idea what is in them. Worse yet, most churches have borrowed their bylaws and church governing documents from their friends. They have cut and pasted their most important and vital church governing documents from other churches. I call this the *"cut-and-paste mentality."*

Churches need to go to experts to draft their documents!

Several years ago, I had my right knee replaced. It was from an old basketball injury that I sustained in the 70s playing in an adult league in college.[1] The injury went virtually untreated until I finally became lame and could no longer function. When it was time to get a knee replacement, I did not go to my dentist. I went to a fabulous orthopedic surgeon.[2] Both had medical degrees. Only one specialized in knee replacements! It was the best decision I ever made. His specialization in zip surgery minimized the damage done to my ligaments and tendons. My recovery time was insanely fast.

What is the point? *Churches need to go to experts to draft their documents.*

I have met many corporate lawyers who want to assist the church. Unfortunately, they don't understand church polity or the faith.

The corporate work done for the church is probably not wrong. It just may not be right.

The corporation might be set up legally but not be at all reflective of the way the church makes decisions or connects to its denomination or overarching governing authority.

Don't go to your dentist to get your knee replacement!

In the same way, I have met many Christian attorneys who want to help their church. However, they are not skilled corporate lawyers. Again, the well-meaning congregant, who happens to be an attorney, is doing his/her church a disservice to try to address the corporate governance reflected in the bylaws. Only a church law authority, who understands both the polity of the church and the corporate laws of the state, can adequately address the issues that must be included in the bylaws of a church. Don't go to your dentist to get your knee replacement! Don't go to your real estate attorney or family law attorney or your general practitioner to have the most vital documents in the history of the church drafted. Find an expert. You will never be sorry.

---

[1] I wish I could say that it was because I was such a star player. Actually, an old high-school nemesis was still holding a grudge from high school and threw a cross-body block into me when I was shooting a lay-up.

[2] Shout out to Dr. Carter, Hampton Roads Orthopedic and Sports Medicine, Hampton Virginia.

USE MULTIPLE WEAPONS!

Protecting Your Assets

MOST CHURCH ASSETS are structured like assets held in your "junk drawer" at home. All assets are sitting in one spot—in one drawer.

In this kind of configuration, one bad legal moment in the life of a church could unnecessarily expose all the assets to liability.

What Churches Need to Consider:

School
Events
Church Operations
Land
Community Care
Youth
Missions

Most church assets are structured like assets held in a junk drawer:
All the assets are held in 1 spot!
All assets could be exposed to a legal action.

Once a church is incorporated properly, it can better protect its assets. A properly organized and structured church should have the largest footprint in the community God is leading them to. The function or reach of the church should not be limited by its structure.

The church does not serve the structure. The structure should serve the church!

Because we live in a litigious society, it is important to isolate different initiatives that might have high risks. It is first and foremost a containment strategy. We recommend using a single-member limited liability company (LLC) to isolate different church initiatives that are vital to the footprint of the church in its community. Each activity can be vigorously pursued without putting all of the assets of the church at risk.

The church does not serve the structure. The structure should serve the church!

Limited liability company law is well established in virtually all states. The incorporated church still governs and controls the LLC. The LLC can enjoy the tax-exempt status of the incorporated church, yet the risk can be isolated and remain in the LLC. With the proper structuring and proper linkage between the church and the LLC, the church gets the best of both worlds: It can maintain control of the LLC but isolate the risk. As the adage says, "What happens in the LLC stays in the LLC."

The separation of assets can provide protection from liability.

DON'T GIVE A NOVICE A GUN!

Proper Selection and Training of the Board

Make sure you have your "Ducks in a Row"!

I WAS CALLED to a meeting in the central part
of the United States to review the corporate

structure of a church and recommend changes if necessary. At the initial meeting of the leadership team and the board of elders, we sat at a round table in a conference room, and the "team" introduced itself. Everything seemed normal until we got to the treasurer. She was a nice and unassuming middle-aged lady. She began her introduction by saying, "I just want to first and foremost thank Pastor X for putting so much faith and trust in me following my release from prison." I looked around the room, scanning the faces, sure that this was just a practical joke of some kind. It wasn't.

At an opportune time, I took the pastor aside. "Tell me about your treasurer," I said.

"Oh, sister XXXXX is really a good person. She and her husband got caught up in a racketeering and money laundering investigation and were sentenced to time in federal prison. But she really didn't do anything wrong and was just an unwitting victim in the whole mess," the pastor replied.

I took extra time to explain to the pastor that *he could not have a convicted felon as his fiduciary officer and treasurer!*

Needless to say, the selection of the leaders of any non-profit, tax-exempt entity is crucial to the long-term success of the organization. A church, by definition, is a non-profit, tax-exempt entity and, as such, enjoys a special status in the laws of the United States and with the IRS. The board of directors (Board) of a tax-exempt entity has special responsibilities[1] called fiduciary duties, which represent the highest standard in the law. Selection of a Board for your church or non-profit organization cannot be determined merely by friendship. This is not an assignment for your golf buddy or your best friend. The fiduciary responsibilities are real and can have serious consequences whether the Board member understands them or not.

The three important "fiduciary responsibilities" of the board are **The Duty of Care, The Duty of Loyalty, and The Duty of Obedience**:

1) *The Duty of Care* requires that decisions be made in good faith but are arrived at through due diligence and being informed of the facts and consequences of the decision.

2) *The Duty of Loyalty* requires that the church/organization has

a written Conflicts of Interest Policy that will require the disclosure of any conflicts and the process for addressing conflicts when they arise.

3) *The Duty of Obedience* essentially requires the Board to comply with the law (local, state, and federal) and to comply with the organization's bylaws.

We regularly conduct non-profit Board training to educate boards of directors on their fiduciary responsibilities. We highly recommend that a firm with a concentration on non-profit and church Board administration be engaged as early and often as possible to conduct an independent review and analysis of the following major categories:

- Board of Trustees Oversight Procedures
- Financial Practices, Statements, and Transactional Disclosures
- Conflicts of Interest
- Human Resources

- Use and Management of Resources

Think about it. We don't let a novice behind the wheel of a car without some training!

You don't give a high-tech weapon to a soldier who has never gone through basic training or qualified on the firing range!

However, non-profit and church Boards are organized every day to handle major assets governed by local, state, and federal laws with no training!

It isn't fair to the leaders and certainly not fair to the congregants who have entrusted the church with their tithes and offerings and resulting assets.

Top 10 Non-Profit Essentials for Boards

We recommend, as a minimum, that non-profit boards be acquainted with the "Top Ten Essentials" for non-profit boards.

Essential areas to be covered include:

1) Determine and Know the Mission and the Purpose
   a. Ensure that the mission is clearly stated and advanced.
   b. Mission: What the organization is and does
   c. Vision: What the organization strives to be and do

2) Select the Chief Executive

3) Support and Evaluate the Chief Executive

  a. Both the chief executive and the Board should do their best to adhere to the doctrine of "no surprises:"

      i.   Personnel problems

      ii. Cash flow

      iii. Contracts

  b. Annual review

      i.   Status and evaluation of goals set

      ii. Compensation

4) Ensure Effective Planning
    a. Financial Planning
    b. Projects
    c. Risk Management
        i.   By failing to assess the threats and challenges honestly, the Board is blindly navigating for the organization.

5) Monitor and Strengthen Programs
    a. Constantly evaluate if programs match the mission and are effective.
    b. Evaluate the cost-benefit ratio.
    c. May need to discontinue a less effective program to implement a new program
        i.   Help foster an environment and culture that embraces change.

6) Ensure Financial Resources

a. Provide adequate resources for the organization to fulfill its mission.

b. Each major project or program should have specific goals and fundraising strategies.

7) Fiduciary Responsibilities

a. Assist in developing the annual budget.

b. Ensure proper financial controls are in place:

    i. Independent annual audit or review

    ii. Consult financial planners

    iii. Internal monitoring

8) Train and Recruit a Competent Board

a. Ongoing Training and Assessment of the Board

    i. Clarify expectations

    ii. Assess board member performance

  iii. Orient new board members

  iv. Provide in-service education

9) Enhance the Organization's Public Image

 a. Someone is always listening and watching.

 b. Discuss and communicate goals and missions accomplished.

 c. Publicize the contribution being made to the community and for the public good.

10) Ensure Legal and Ethical Integrity:

 a. Have regularly scheduled Legal Compliance Audits to ensure you have your ducks in a row.

[1] Luke 12:48 (AMP) "From everyone to whom much has been given, much will be required; and to whom they entrusted much, of him they will ask all the more."

WHO OWNS THE SERMON?

Intellectual Property Rights for Resources

ONE OF THE MOST frequent questions that arise in my non-profit and church law practice is the issue of the ownership of intellectual property.

Today's pastors and church leaders have a much broader and more diverse ministry footprint than was ever imagined before. It is not unusual for a pastor to develop for his local church on Sunday a tremendous series on an important spiritual subject. It has traction, and the pastor is asked to speak at a seminar. He has the sermon copied onto a CD and packaged in an attractive series set. He then offers the series for sale at seminars.

Who gets the money?

I know you are going to roll your eyes, but the accurate answer is, "It depends." The issue is intertwined with the important IRS prohibition against Private Inurement. *Private inurement* is when a 501(c)(3) nonprofit's money is devoted to *private* uses instead of charitable purposes. Obviously, this requirement is not satisfied where a nonprofit's money is used to benefit insiders instead of furthering its exempt purposes.

The good news is that there are at least three valid ways to address this situation. Each depends on education, intentionality, and expert planning on the part of the pastor, the church, the legal team, and the accountants.

Scenario 1: The church owns the sermon.

The pastor has created the sermon on church time, with church resources, as part of his primary job description.[1] In this instance, any money generated from the series should be directed to the church. Otherwise, the pastor could be in danger of violating the IRS prohibition against Private Inurement.

Scenario 2: *The church owns the sermon, and the Pastor licenses it.*

In this instance, the pastor can pay fair market value for the sermon, including all expenses to produce the CD and packaging. Many churches recognize the value to the church of the exposure and experience of their pastor speaking in conferences and leadership forums. The church is free to license the use of the sermon to the pastor. By paying fair market value for the resource, the pastor can then use the sermon and charge a retail price for the resource. The wholesale value goes back to the church, and the pastor keeps the balance. This is heavily dependent on both a proper job description being drafted for the pastor and a proper license agreement being drafted between the pastor and the church.

Scenario 3: *The pastor owns the sermon.*

A fair number of my clients elect to develop their sermons on their own time. Their job descriptions permit them to have significant time away from their normal church duties. They develop their sermons on their own time, using their own resources, and speak at conferences,[2] seminars, and leadership forums. They then bring their sermons back to the church. In this instance, they own their sermons. Any money paid for this resource belongs to the pastor.

---

[1] A well-drafted job description can allow the pastor to serve not only the local church, but also ministry at large to other congregations, meetings, and seminars. This is vital if the pastor has a ministry beyond the local church.

[2] In these instances, we regularly set up both 1). A non-profit, tax-exempt ministry for the pastor (Pastor Ministry, Inc.) and 2). A for-profit entity (Pastor Enterprises, LLC) for those pastors who are creating books and resources that cross-over to the secular marketplace.

DON'T OVERHEAT THE WEAPONS!

IRS Hot Spots: Private Inurement and Excess Compensation

THE IRS GIVES particular focus to the following important areas: the issue of *Private Inurement* and the issue of *Excess Compensation.* The issue of Private Inurement has already been referenced.

However, because of the sensitivity of this issue, one additional application of the principal needs to be addressed under Private Inurement.

A non-profit, tax-exempt entity is not owned by anyone. In its most elemental form, it is a public trust, held for its stated tax-exempt purpose[1], governed by a Board. This means that the pastor cannot own a church. If a church property is deeded in the name of a pastor, such a structure would violate the IRS prohibition against Private Inurement and would void the tax-exempt status of the church and result in fines and onerous penalties.

The issue of Excess Compensation is another delicate matter that is especially sensitive to the IRS. If the leader of a non-profit, tax-exempt organization is being paid an excessive amount as determined by an IRS audit, then that executive must disgorge the excess and usually pay fines and penalties. The Board, who allows the executive to have been paid Excess Compensation, can also be fined. If the parties do not respond properly to the IRS on this issue, the tax-exempt status of the organization can be revoked.[2]

How do you know if you have violated the IRS prohibition against Excess Compensation? The good news is that the IRS has provided a mechanism for compliance in this area called an *"Independent Compensation Study"*.

The Board may commission an independent company to conduct an Independent

Compensation Study that properly identifies the range of compensation appropriate for the executive(s). This will be based on metrics such as the education of the executive, assets under management, demographics of the region, cost-of-living index, and other comparable data from other similar organizations. If the Board relies on this study in setting the executive compensation, then the Board has what is called a *"Safe Harbor"* against the fines and penalties that are normally levied against them personally and against the organization.[3]

---

[1] For instance, the Tax-Exempt Purpose of a church can be for the establishment of religion and the worldwide dissemination of the Gospel. Under this purpose, the poor can be helped, the hungry fed, children schooled in religious instruction, worldwide missions funded, etc.

[2] This would also entail every donor having to amend their tax returns. Their reported donations would no longer be exempt—kind of a non-starter for most donors!

---

[3] The Compensation Study must be conducted by an independent third party, such as a law firm, a CPA, or a company regularly engaged in this area. We have conducted such studies for clients in many parts of the United States.

Choose Your Ammunition!

Ministry vs. Church

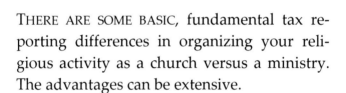

THERE ARE SOME BASIC, fundamental tax reporting differences in organizing your religious activity as a church versus a ministry. The advantages can be extensive.

Church

Churches receive their tax-exempt status by virtue of the Constitution of the United States. Churches are automatically tax exempt. They do not need to file for Recognition of Exemption with the IRS. However, many of our clients take an extra step and file the IRS Form 1023 or 1023-EZ to obtain the official *"Determination Letter"* from the IRS.

This can help with immigration issues and also with state and local tax matters. However, churches do not have to file Form 990 on an annual basis. Only churches are exempt from filing this Form 990.

The term *church* is found, but not specifically defined, in the Internal Revenue Code. With the exception of the special rules for church audits, the use of the term *church* also includes conventions and associations of churches as well as the integrated auxiliaries of a church.

Certain characteristics are generally attributed to churches and have been devel-

oped by the IRS and by court decisions. They
include:

- Distinct legal existence
- Recognized creed and form of
  worship
- Definite and distinct
  ecclesiastical government
- Formal code of doctrine and
  discipline
- Distinct religious history
- Membership not associated with
  any other church or
  denomination
- Organization of ordained
  ministers
- Ordained ministers selected
  after completing prescribed
  courses of study
- Literature of its own
- Established places of worship
- Regular congregations
- Regular religious services
- Sunday schools for the religious
  instruction of the young
- Schools for the preparation of its
  members

The IRS generally uses a combination of these characteristics, together with other facts and circumstances, to determine whether an organization is considered a church for federal tax purposes.

Ministry

Ministries must demonstrate that they fulfill a tax-exempt purpose under IRS Section 501(c)(3). IRS.gov lists the following definition of requirements for tax-exemption:

> To be tax-exempt under section 501(c)(3) of the Internal Revenue Code, an organization must be **organized** and **operated** exclusively for **exempt purposes** set forth in section 501(c)(3), and none of its earnings may **inure** to any private shareholder or individual. In addition, it may not be an *action organization, i.e.,* it may not attempt to influence legislation as a substantial part of its activities and it may not participate in any campaign activity for or against political candidates.

The exempt purposes set forth in section 501(c) (3) are charitable, religious, educational, scientific, literary, testing for public safety, fostering national or international amateur sports competition, and preventing cruelty to children or animals. The term *charitable* is used in its generally accepted legal sense and includes relief of the poor, the distressed, or the under-privileged; advancement of religion; advancement of education or science; erecting or maintaining public buildings, monuments, or works; lessening the burdens of government; lessening neighbor-hood tensions; eliminating prejudice and discrimination; defending human and civil rights secured by law; and combating community deterioration and juvenile delin-quency.[1]

For a ministry to be recognized as a tax-exempt entity, it must file a Form 1023 or Form 1023-EZ with the IRS. The process can take up to six months. Once recognized as a tax-exempt entity, a ministry must file a form 990 annually with the IRS. (Churches are not required to make an annual filing).

---

[1] www.irs.gov/charities-non-profits

THINK PAST LUNCH!

*Leadership Transitions and Succession
Planning for Pastors*

I BELIEVE GOD THINKS GENERATIONALLY. He is
the God of Abraham, Isaac, and Jacob – three
generations. A good leader must consider
succession. A good leader must "think past
lunch."

The corporate mechanism that can make
or break an organization is the bylaws. This
crucial document cannot be borrowed from a
friend. The future stability of your organization—your church—depends on bylaws that
accurately reflect not only how decisions are
made in the church, but how the church will
handle transition. The bylaws will identify
the trip wires that will either initiate transi-

tions in leadership or govern transitions as they happen.

Transition—a kind word for disruption or change—is going to happen in every company, and in every church!

Well-drafted bylaws should address Board selection, officer selection, and voting [how decisions are made among the church membership and the leaders]. Proper bylaws should also identify predictable scenarios that have arisen in the life of churches and non-profit organizations, such as the retirement of the pastor; disability of the pastor; death of the pastor; malfeasance; discipline; and removal for cause. If a change is going to happen, it needs to happen in the most orderly and least disruptive and destructive way possible.

In my former corporate life, as head of advertising sales worldwide for the Family Channel, I was responsible for managing the sales forces in New York, Chicago, Los Angeles, Detroit, London, and Hong Kong. We had many moving parts, but I always considered managing transition as one of my main jobs. Transition—a kind word for disruption or change—is going to happen in every company, and in every church. The question is not if change is going to happen, but when and how. The mechanisms contained in the bylaws can minimize the disruption change can cause in the church. The bylaws can make the difference between change that destroys the church and change that is annoying and uncomfortable but is managed as positively as possible.

Don't leave this crucial document to an amateur. Only entrust this important part of your church history and future to experts.

ARMOR 9

FORMULATE AN EXIT PLAN

Estate Planning for Pastors and Congregants

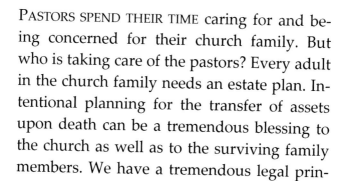

PASTORS SPEND THEIR TIME caring for and be-ing concerned for their church family. But who is taking care of the pastors? Every adult in the church family needs an estate plan. In-tentional planning for the transfer of assets upon death can be a tremendous blessing to the church as well as to the surviving family members. We have a tremendous legal prin-ciple available to us in America called *"Free-dom of Disposition"*.

At the outset, the founding fathers decid-ed it was in the best interest of society as a whole to incentivize individuals and families to build generational wealth. The best way to do that was to ensure every person that they could pass their estates to anyone they wished. No one has a right to inherit our estate in America, but we have the right to give our estate to anyone.

This Freedom of Disposition is a bedrock principle in America. We should focus on and care about the transfer of our estate. It can be a tremendous blessing to the church to be named as a beneficiary of a portion of our estates. As under-shepherds, pastors have the opportunity to encourage their congregants to have estate plans and to take advantage of this wonderful principle in American law. This is especially true with the elderly in our churches.

The Silver Tsunami

Nothing is more important than addressing the estate planning needs of the elderly. We are facing what sociologists called the *"Silver Tsunami in America"*.

People are living longer than ever. Seniors are predicted to live much longer than their parents and grandparents. However, the rapidly growing senior population has been likened to a *catastrophic storm*. New pressure is being brought to bear in every area of health care due to this rising demographic shift. Many experts project the number of people over the age of 65 to double over the next 25 years. This is good news for many of us 55 and over. However, there has never been more urgency to address estate planning, especially for seniors.

The best time to do estate planning, and especially to address emergency situations, is now — while you can. Many times, you will not get a second chance!

The issue is really centered on *"capacity"*. The nagging truth is that *all planning stops* when a person loses the capacity to make a legal decision. Memory issues like dementia or medical events like a stroke or disabling injury can affect legal capacity. When legal capacity is lost, all planning opportunities stop; doctors can't talk to you; and access to medical records is denied. Your family and trusted friends can no longer admit or discharge you from medical facilities. The only recourse left at that point is expensive, time-consuming, and sometimes embarrassing public hearings to authorize your family and loved ones to assist you.

The best time to do estate planning, and especially to address emergency situations, is now—while you can. Many times, you will not get a second chance!

What Does Estate Planning Consist Of?

The minimal estate planning process should consist of:

1) **Reviewing and Updating Current Estate Planning Documents**
   a. Reviewing existing estate planning documents to make sure they reflect your current wishes
   b. Reviewing out-of-state documents to ensure compliance with local state laws
   c. Updating and/or executing new estate planning documents, which include wills, trusts, powers of

attorney, and advanced medical directives.

2) Financial Well-Being & Planning Check-Up

a. Evaluating current assets and sources of income and assessing whether additional support may be available

b. Evaluating various options for paying long-term care, including insurance, Veteran's benefits, Medicaid, or reverse mortgages.

c. Maximizing benefits and resources available to a spouse who remains at home when the other spouse enters a long-term care facility

3) Housing

a. Offering guidance on various options for housing and assessments that may be passed down by the family

b. Evaluating various options for in-home long-term care solutions

An expert estate planning attorney should share your unique and valuable passion and acknowledge your hard work to see your family taken care of. Throughout life, various adjustments must be made to succeed in this mission. Adjustments become imperative not only to the success of your financial well-being but that of your parents, children, and grandchildren.

True estate planning attorneys are not document salesmen but are professionals dedicated to focusing on your story and your unique family needs.

As an adjunct law school professor with a concentration in trusts and estates, I urge you to trust your estate planning to experts only. True estate planning attorneys are not document salesmen but are professionals dedicated to focusing on your story and your unique family needs. It has been my privilege to help clients navigate the various hurdles that life can suddenly bring and commit to educating the client and family and exhausting every possible option. Find an expert in this area. The future disposition of your estate is too important to trust to the inexperienced or generalist. I have ushered my own parents into heaven and now am in the phase of ensuring my family has a clear path and plan. Find someone who is dedicated to developing meaningful and usable strategies for assisting clients to preserve, protect, and effectively pass on wealth and their legacy.[1]

---

[1] We don't presume that every reader will use our firm, but it would certainly be our privilege to share with you the different strategies we have learned. Please feel free to contact me at *slentzesq@gmail.com.*

ARMOR 10

DON'T GO TO WAR ALONE!

Take an Army with You

IN MY CORPORATE CAREER, I have had the privilege of conducting business on seven continents. In my law practice, I have the honor of representing clients in all 50 states and several countries. The reason I have had any measure of success working in multiple jurisdictions is my understanding, appreciation, and respect for the value and need for a team. I like the *New Living Translation* of Luke 14:28:

> But don't begin until you count the cost. For who would begin construction of a building without

first calculating the cost to see if
there is enough money to finish it?

In my opinion, the cost of having a viable church that will stand the test of time is assembling not only a good congregation but also the right business team. I believe the short-term and long-term success of a church or an organization is directly related to the urgency and emphasis that it places on assembling a viable business team as early as possible in its development. Frank Demazio, a trusted church planter and leader, puts it this way: "The church is a living organism that must find its life and power applied through organization and structure."[1]

Do not try to form and run a church without identifying and enlisting the support of at least three key players who can guide the organization and structure of the church:

1) Your spouse
2) An expert church law attorney
3) An expert accountant who understands non-profit/church management

To the extent that any of these elements are missing, the organization is headed for trouble.

Number (1) goes without saying. If your spouse is not supportive and in agreement with your vision to pastor a church, I highly recommend that you rethink your calling! That said, it is essential that you have legal and accounting advice throughout the history of your organization. If you feel you can't afford it, then I question whether you should be doing it at all.

Lives, fortunes, destinies, and souls depend on us getting this right. We owe it to the generations to come to organize and structure our churches for success!

---

1 http://www.frankdamazio.com/2012/05/team-structure/

About the Author

Stephen D. Lentz, Esq.
Slentzesq@gmail.com
757-288-9240
www.StephenDLentz.com

STEPHEN D. LENTZ is recognized as one of the top five church law authorities in the U.S., representing denominations and churches in all 50 states and every province in Canada.

He is the founding attorney of Lentz Law Group. Steve guided his firm to become a boutique business and estate planning practice, serving clients in the areas of corporate formation, complex business transactions, entertainment law, intellectual property, nonprofit law, foundation and church/ministry representation, simple and complex estate planning, and elder law. He has counseled corporations and non-profit organizations in the United States and around the world.

In addition to his legal practice, Steve serves as adjunct professor at Regent University School of Law, where he has taught Wills, Trusts & Estates, Law Practice Management, International Business Transactions, Intellectual Property and Entertainment Law. He also served as adjunct faculty of Regent University's Graduate School of Communications, where he taught Media Law, Policy, and Ethics.

Prior to establishing the Lentz Law Group in Tidewater, Virginia, Steve spent 15 years in the television industry. From 1997 to 2000, he was the President of Middle East Television, responsible for crafting the legal strategy to change the commercial broadcast laws in Israel. This would permit non-Israeli television entities to run advertising targeted at Israel. Middle East Television became the largest super-station in the Middle East, reaching a potential audience of over 100 million viewers in 17 Arab countries and all of Israel. Steve functioned as in-house counsel and appeared either in person or by counsel before the Israeli Supreme Court six times in the 14 months prior to 1999.

From 1993 to 1997, Steve was the President and CEO of Fit TV and was instrumental in building the company into an attractive national niche cable network. As in-house counsel, he was responsible for both employment and television broadcast law compliance as well as entertainment contracts. During this time, he regularly dealt with issues related to interstate commercial law and emerging cyber-law issues. He helped craft the strategy to sell the company to Fox Sports in 1997.

From 1985 to 1993, Steve was the Senior Vice President of Worldwide Sales for International Family Entertainment (better known as The Family Channel), where he managed advertising sales offices in New York, Chicago, Detroit, Los Angeles, London, and Hong Kong. He was part of the strategic management team that led to International Family Entertainment's successful IPO and later sale to Rupert Murdoch for $1.8 billion.

Licenses and Awards:

- Supreme Court of Virginia, Virginia State Bar
- Supreme Court of Tennessee, Tennessee State Bar
- Professional Affiliations, Awards, and Service
- Virginia Bar Association
- Business Law Section
- Corporate Counsel Section
- Trusts & Estates Section
- Adjunct Faculty, Regent University School of Law
- Wills, Trusts, & Estates; Entertainment Law; International Business Transactions, Business Associations, Law Practice Management
- Adjunct Faculty: Regent University Graduate School of Communications
- Media Law, Policy, & Ethics

- 2017–2018 Top Lawyers of Coastal Virginia, *COVABIZ Magazine*, January 2018
- 2018–2019 Top Lawyers of Coastal Virginia, *COVABIZ Magazine*, January 2019